How to make
WILD ANIMALS

Jane Gisby

SEARCH PRESS

Introduction

Everybody loves animals, and soft, furry toys have a special place in the hearts of many children — adults find them irresistable too! My own interest in animals began at a very early age when I was lucky enough to be able to pay frequent, often daily visits, to the superb zoological gardens in Bristol. I'll never forget the day that an uncle adopted one of the monkeys as a special birthday present for me — but even that does not compare with the thrill of seeing an animal in its natural surroundings. Today, there are many beautiful nature books and wildlife documentaries that teach us about the animal and enable us to see it in its native habitat.

The soft toy animals in this book are easy to make and I have designed them to be as appealing and as durable as possible. The latter is especially important because a favourite toy can be in constant demand and is often loved to bits! Even when the child has grown up, the treasured toy increases in sentimental value and is lovingly tucked away, ready for the next generation.

It is fun to create a toy that will bring such joy and pleasure and I hope you get as much happiness out of making these animals as I have had in designing them.

Materials and methods

Choice of fabrics

A wide range of fur fabrics is now available to enable the toy maker to create realistic wild animals. Some furs are described in catalogues as being suitable for certain animals, but often a particular fabric can be suitable for several quite different creatures.

Always choose a good quality fur with a firm backing which cannot be seen when the pile is flattened for inspection. An inferior fabric will create a disappointing toy. Soft toys for babies or young children should be washable and made from fur with a short dense pile; fabric with a medium or long pile can be made into toys for older children or adults.

Felt must also be of good quality, otherwise it will wear out before the fur fabric of the body. Small shapes are easier to cut out if non-toxic glue is first spread on to the back of the felt and then allowed to dry.

Check that fabrics used are fire retardant.

Equipment

No special equipment is required for making toys at home, but it helps to check that you have everything you need before beginning a project.

A sewing machine gives a strong even finish to seams; however, a hand sewn back stitch seam can be used instead. Matching sewing and strong threads, plus a contrast thread (for sewing marks) are required. A long needle is needed to mould the head; sharp pointed scissors to cut fur fabric and a flat surface on which to work.

See 'Preparing the patterns' below for detailed requirements.

Preparing the patterns

To make the patterns you need dressmakers' graph or plain paper, thin card, a pencil, rule, set square and envelope. Use the dressmakers' graph paper, or draw an accurate grid on to the paper, using a rule and set square.

The patterns are shown on a grid, the squares of which must be drawn to the size given for each different animal. Carefully plot the printed pattern on to the enlarged grid. Clearly name each pattern piece and mark it with sewing instructions. To make a whole pattern (where applicable) fold a piece of paper in half and place the centre broken line of the enlarged pattern on to the fold. Draw round the outside of the pattern, cut out the double paper and open the whole pattern. Glue the paper patterns to card, or redraw them on to card and cut them out. Cut out the required number of each pattern piece from scrap paper; for example, two legs, four ears, etc. Keep the patterns for each toy in their own envelope, or string them together.

Cutting out

Before cutting out any pieces, mark the direction of the pile on the back of the fabric; lay all the patterns out on the wrong side of the fabric, to ensure that they will fit. Seams are allowed. Remember to reverse one of each pattern (where indicated) to make a pair and check the pile on the reversed pieces. The arrows on the patterns indicate the fur pile or nap.

Cut the fur backing with scissor points to avoid bald seams. Use a needle and contrasting colour thread to take short separate basting stitches through the fabric backing to mark the sewing instructions.

Stitching

Matching sewing and strong threads plus a contrast thread(for sewing marks) are required for making all the toys. 8 mm (1/3 in) seams are allowed for the large toys and 5 mm (1/5 in) seams for the smaller toys.

The seams are made on the wrong side of the fabric, (right side facing). If pins are used to hold parts together, they should be long with a coloured head. Count the number used to ensure that none remain in the toy.

Oversew the raw edges, to keep the fur from moving, then stitch the seam. Oversew the edges of bodies which are left open for turning. When stitching is completed, the fabric is turned to the right side; narrow parts, such as tails, can be eased through with a wooden spoon handle, or something similar.

Ladder stitch is used for closing up the gaps after filling and also for attaching parts, ears and tails etc. to the toy's body. Use a matching strong thread. Secure the thread with the back stitches in the seam allowance. Make a small running stitch on the seam line on one edge. Take the needle across the opening and make a small stitch on the opposite edge of the gap. Continue with several stitches on alternative edges, then pull up the thread and the raw edges will be turned to the inside out of sight. At the end of the stitching the thread must be firmly secured.

prevent eyes and noses from being pulled through the fabric.

The stalks for the plastic eyes and noses are pushed through the prepared holes, from the right side, and the washers forced down the stalks as far as possible. Once so placed, it is almost impossible to remove them without tearing the fabric, or breaking the washer. Accurate placing is therefore most important. You can hold the eyes on to the completed filled head before making the holes and choose a suitable or different look for each toy. The filling is then removed and the eyes fixed in position.

Mouths, (and noses), can also be embroidered with satin and straight stitches, using fine yarn or embroidery thread. To embroider a mouth for the bears, mark the shape of the mouth with pins. Make straight stitches between the pins, or take one long stitch for the mouth which is fastened to the fur fabric by single stitches at the base of each pin, (see Fig 1). Remove the pins.

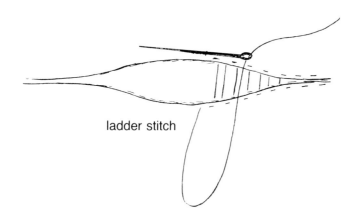

ladder stitch

Eyes, noses and mouths

Eyes and noses can be made from felt and stitched on to the fabric; this is preferable when making toys for babies and young children as they seem to find plastic features extremely pleasant to chew!

If you are using plastic eyes and noses, these must conform to approved safety standards. Tiny slits made in the fur fabric for plastic features are oversewn round the edges to

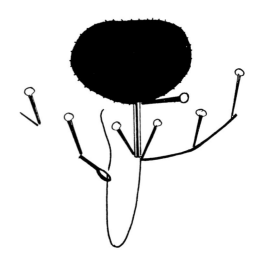

fig 1 to embroider a mouth for the bears

To embroider a mouth and nose for the lion, tiger and leopard, use straight stitch and sew as shown opposite, (see Fig 2.) The lion's eye markings are made with black and white permanent waterproof marking pens, (see Fig 3).

4

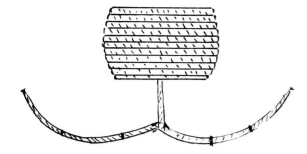

fig 2   to embroider a nose and mouth for the lion, tiger and leopard

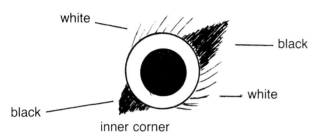

white

black

black

white

inner corner

fig 3   lion's eye markings

The monkey's nose is embroidered with small straight stitches. The seam line marks the mouth, (see Fig 4). The Orang-Outang's features are accentuated by marking the mouth, and areas around the eyes, with a brown permanent waterproof marker pen.

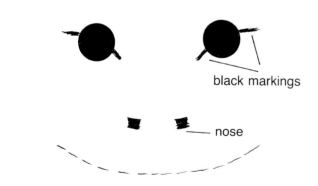

black markings

nose

fig 4   monkey's face

Filling

Materials for filling should be clean, light and washable, if the toy is for a baby or small child. Polyester fibre, which is available in very soft and also heavier grades, is the most popular. The softer the filling, the lighter and more cuddly the toy.

Check that the filling used is flame retardant

Finishing

Use the eye of a needle to release any fur pile caught in seam stitches, taking special care round the ears, paws and feet. If required, the pile can be trimmed round the eyes and nose, using small pointed scissors. Do not cut too close to the backing, as this can easily create a straight clipped line in the pile, or expose the fabric. Brush the fur lightly in the direction of the pile.

The expression of the face can alter the whole toy. The way in which the eyes and ears are set will largely determine whether the toy looks fierce or friendly and you may need to experiment to obtain the results which please you most.

To alter the set of the eyes, you can use a long needle and strong thread. Take a stitch from the inner eye, through the head, to behind the opposite ear. Pull the thread and see if you like the resulting expression. If you do, then make a second stitch before fastening the thread securely behind the ear. Make the same adjustment to the other eye.

Stitches taken across the lower front head gusset can shape the bridge of the nose (see the lion on page 25); a stitch made across the base of the ears will curve or bring them forward.

Safety

Safety is of paramount importance when making toys — whether they are intended as gifts or for bazaar sales. All materials — fabrics, fillings and features must conform to officially recognized safety standards and the first two must be *flame retardant*. Do not use buttons as eyes on toys for babies! All small parts must be *firmly* sewn to the body. Squeakers and growlers, if used, should be enclosed in a small muslin bag and sewn firmly to the inside of the toy's fabric.

Bears

Koalas, pandas, a brown bear and a polar bear are shown in this section. The koala bears and small panda are made from separate patterns. The larger bears are adapted from the same basic body pattern, but different head patterns are used for each animal.

Koala Bears

To make the large and small koala bears, use the patterns shown on pages 8 and 9. The pattern for the large bear should be drawn on to a 5 cms (2 ins) grid to give a height of 33 cms (13 ins); the pattern for the small bear should be drawn on to a 3 cms (1¼ ins) grid to give a height of 23 cms (9 ins).

Materials

For one large and one small bear:
Medium pile fawn fur fabric, 30 × 138 cms (11¾ × 54⅜ ins).
Medium pile white fur fabric, (the pile to be stroked down towards the shorter length of both the white and fawn fabrics), 30 × 64 cms (11¾ × 25¼ ins).
Black felt, 24 × 24 cms (9½ × 9½ ins).
1 pair 18 mm and 1 pair 9 mm brown safety eyes and washers.
670 gm (1½ lb) polyester filling.
Handicraft glue.
Squared paper, 5 cms (2 ins) and 3 cms (1¼ ins).

Patterns

The following twelve pattern pieces are required, enlarged on to a 5 cms (2 ins) grid for the large bear, or on to a 3 cms (1¼ ins) grid for the small bear — front head, back head, snout, nose, inner ear, outer ear, body, front body, base, inner arm, inner leg, paw.

Cutting out

The seam allowance for the large bear is 8 mm ⅓ in); for the small bear it is 5 mm (⅕ ins). Arrows indicate direction of pile. For each bear cut out the following pattern pieces:
From fawn fur fabric cut 1 pair front heads, 1 pair back heads; 1 snout; 1 pair outer ears; 1 pair bodies; 1 base.
From white fur fabric cut 1 front body; 1 pair inner arms; 1 pair inner legs; 1 pair inner ears.
Fold the black felt in half and glue, or bond the two layers together, cut out 1 nose and 4 paws.

To make

All seams are made with right sides facing.
1. Stitch darts in front heads.
2. Stitch front heads together A-B.
3. Stitch darts in snout.
4. Stitch snout to front heads C-B-C.
5. In a continuous seam, stitch snout seam E-C, tapering the stitches at E and the front heads together C-D.
6. Make a tiny slit through the dart at the eye position. Insert the eye from the right side and secure with the washer. Repeat for the second eye.
7. Stitch back heads together A-G.
8. Stitch inner arms to the front body H-J.
9. Stitch inner legs to the front body K-L.
10. Stitch dart in front body.
11. Stitch base to front body L-L.
12. Stitch darts in bodies and oversew centre back edges between dots.
13. Stitch bodies together G-N, leaving seam open between dots.

Koala bears live in the eucalyptus forests of Australia. They are mainly nocturnal and although they do travel on the ground, they prefer to spend their lives up in the trees where they are more agile. Their chief food is the bark and leaf of the eucalyptus tree. Although in the last century koala populations were decimated by forest fires, hunting and land clearance, today, due to intensive management, they are relatively common in their native habitat.

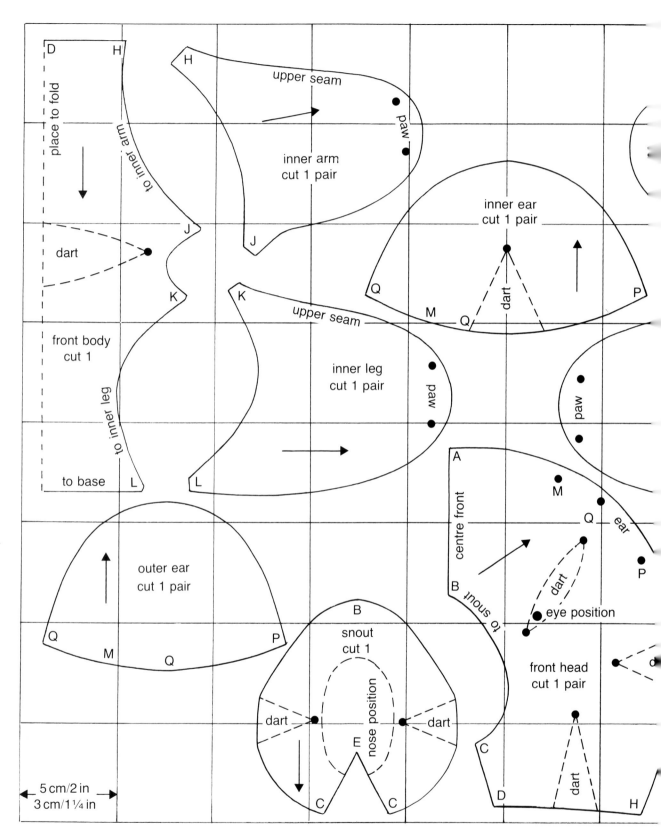

Pattern for large and small koala bears

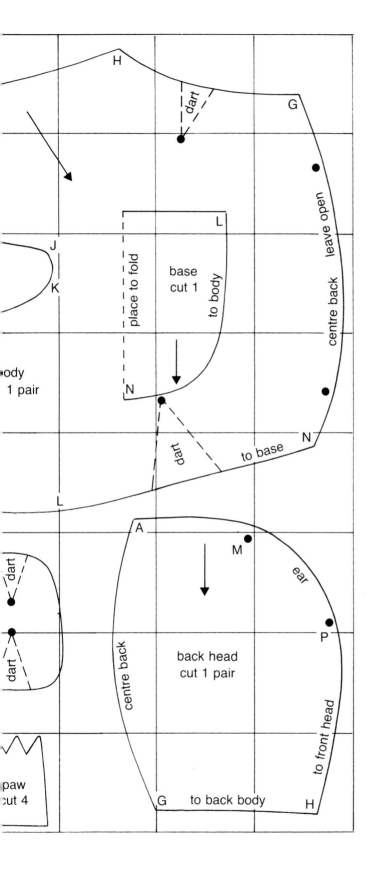

14. Stitch front head to front body H-D-H.
15. Stitch back head to body H-G-H.
16. Stitch darts in inner ears. Stitch one inner ear to one outer ear leaving open curved edge Q-M-Q-P. Turn ear to right side and baste open edges together. Make the second ear in the same way.
17. Fold one ear, with inner ears facing, at M matching Q to Q. Baste the ear to the right side of the front head M-Q-P with raw edges even and the fold of the ear towards the centre head. Repeat, folding the second ear at the opposite curved edge.
18. Stitch round the edge of the paws. Baste paws to the front body at the arms and legs, with the thumbs to the centre.
19. Baste the front of the koala to the back round the head and the limbs, matching A (top of head)-H-J-K-L (lower leg). Check that the raw edges are even at the ears and paws. Baste the base to the body L-N (centre back seam)-L. Stitch the seam round the whole bear. Turn the body through to the right side.
20. Stitch darts in nose. Trim excess felt at the darts and press seam open with thumb.
21. Fill the toy, taking care to mould the nose and head to a good shape.
22. Turn in raw edges of centre back opening and sew the edges of the gap together to enclose filling.
23. By hand, oversew the nose to the snout, adding a little filling before completing the stitching.
24. Run a needle along the seams to release any caught fur.

9

Small panda

To make the small panda, use the pattern shown on page 13. This should be drawn on to a 2.5 cms (1 in) grid, to give a height of 23 cms (9 ins).

Materials

Medium pile black fur fabric, 18 × 60 cms (7 × 23½ ins).
Medium pile white fur fabric, (the pile to be stroked down towards the shorter length of both the black and white fabrics), 20 × 40 cms (7¾ × 15¾ ins).
Black felt, 4 × 8 cms (1½ × 3¼ ins).
1 pair 9 mm brown safety eyes and washers.
Black embroidery thread.
110 gm (4 oz) polyester filling.
Squared paper, 2.5 cms (1 in).

Patterns

The following 11 pattern pieces are required, enlarged on to a 2.5 cms (1 in) grid — upper front body, upper back body, lower front body, lower back body, leg, head, head gusset, neck gusset, ear, eye patch, nose.

Cutting out

The seam allowance is 5 mm (⅕ in). Arrows indicate direction of pile.
Cut out the following pattern pieces:
From the black fur cut 1 pair upper front bodies; 1 pair upper back bodies; 2 pairs legs; 4 ears.
From white fur cut 1 pair heads; 1 head gusset; 1 neck gusset; 1 pair lower front bodies; 1 pair lower back bodies.
Spread glue on to the back of felt, allow to dry before cutting 1 pair eye patches; 1 nose.

To make

All seams are made with right sides facing.
1. Stitch dart in upper front bodies.
2. Stitch upper front body to lower front body A-B. Repeat with the other two pieces.
3. Stitch front bodies together C-A-D.
4. Stitch upper back body to lower back body C-B. Repeat with the other two pieces.
5. Oversew edges of each back body between dots. Stitch back bodies together F-C-D, leaving open between dots.
6. Stitch front to back body, round the arm and lower body from G (at neck)-B-E on both sides, leaving open front and back neck edges (G-J-C-J-G) and (G-K-F-K-G).
7. Stitch bodies together E-D-E.
8. Stitch head gusset to neck gusset H-H.
9. Stitch darts in neck edge of heads.
10. Stitch head and neck gusset to both head pieces J-H-K.
11. With right sides facing stitch head into neck matching C (at front)-J-G-K-F (back) on both sides of the body. Turn panda through to right side.
12. Oversew edges of legs between dots. Stitch the legs together in pairs leaving open between dots. Turn legs to right side.
13. Stitch ears together in pairs, leaving open straight edges. Turn to right side, fold in raw edges and slip stitch together.
14. Place eye patches on to head. Trim fur pile under patches and sew the patches to the head.
15. Make a tiny slit through the patches and fabric for the eyes. Insert the eyes and secure with the washers.
16. Trim the fur pile round the nose. Sew nose in position at H. Embroider mouth.
17. Fill the panda, moulding the head to a good shape. Turn in the open raw edges of the back and oversew to enclose filling.

Giant pandas live high up in the damp, cool bamboo forests of central and west China. Their principle food is the bamboo, although in the wild they will also eat grasses, bulbs and occasionally small animals and insects. They are one of the rarest animals known today. Because of this rarity and the inaccessibility of the bamboo thickets, little is known about the pandas' habits in the wild. Their endearing and cuddly appearance makes them a great favourite and they have become increasingly popular since their discovery in 1869.

18. Fill legs, turn in raw edges and oversew to close. With strong thread sew the legs to the lower body.
19. Sew the ears to the head on placement line. Mould the head by taking a stitch from the inner corner of each eye to behind the opposite ear.
20. Run a needle along seams to release any caught fur.

Large panda

All the large bears are adapted from the same basic body pattern, see pages 14–17, but different head patterns are used.

To make the large panda, use the two patterns shown on the above pages. These should be drawn on to a 5 cms (2 ins) grid, to give a height of 46 cms (18 ins).

Materials

Medium pile black fur fabric, 40 × 130 cms (15¾ × 51¼ ins).

Medium pile white fur fabric (the pile to be stroked down towards the shorter length of both black and white fabrics), 50 × 60 cms (19¾ × 23½ ins).

Black felt, 8 × 8 cms (3¼ × 3¼ ins).

1 pair 21 mm brown safety eyes and washers.

1 kg (2¼ lb) polyester filling.

Handicraft glue.

Squared paper, 5 cms (2 ins).

12

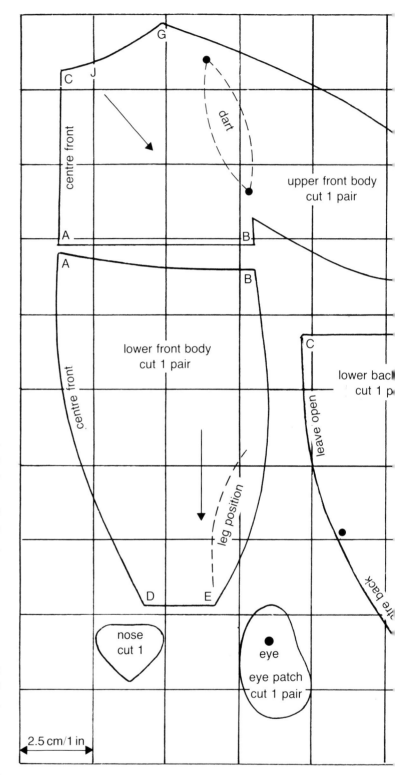

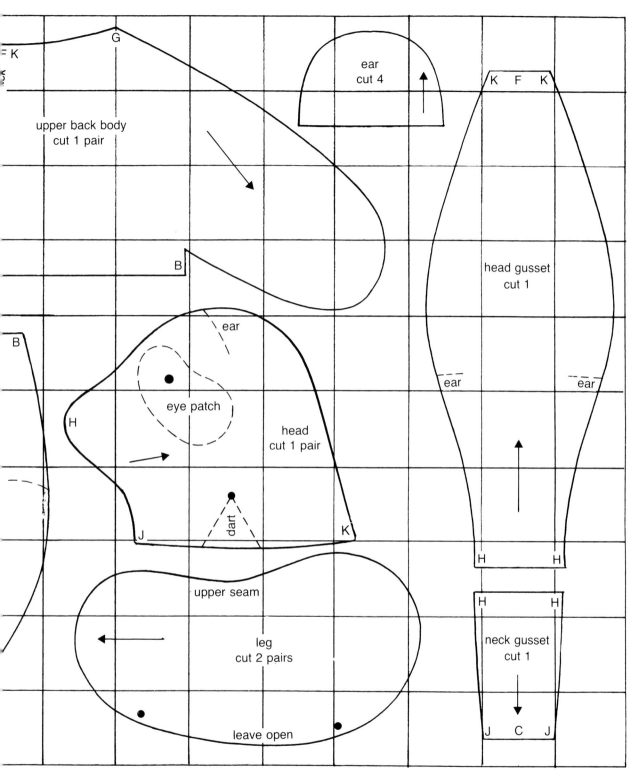

K

G

upper back body
cut 1 pair

ear
cut 4

K F K

B

head gusset
cut 1

B

ear

H

eye patch

head
cut 1 pair

ear

ear

dart

J

K

H

H

upper seam

H

H

neck gusset
cut 1

leg
cut 2 pairs

leave open

J C J

Pattern for small panda

13

Patterns

The following 14 pattern pieces are required, enlarged on to a 5 cms (2 ins) grid — front head No.1, back head No.2, eye patch No.3, head gusset No.4, neck gusset No.5, ear No.6, nose No.7, upper front body No.8, upper back body No.9, lower front body No.10, lower back body No.11, inner leg No.12, outer leg No.13, foot No.14.

Cutting out

The seam allowance is 8 mm (⅓ in). Arrows indicate direction of pile.

Cut out the following pattern pieces: From white fur fabric cut 1 pair front heads; 1 pair back heads; 1 pair lower front bodies; 1 pair lower back bodies; 1 head gusset; 1 neck gusset. From the black fur fabric cut 1 pair upper front bodies; 1 pair upper back bodies; 1 pair eye patches; 1 pair inner legs; 1 pair outer legs; 2 feet; 4 ears.

Spread glue on to the back of the felt, allow to dry, then cut 1 nose.

To make

All seams are made with right sides facing.

First step — the body.

1. Stitch darts in upper front bodies. Stitch upper front bodies together F-G.
2. Stitch upper back bodies together H-J.
3. Stitch lower front bodies together G-L.
4. Oversew raw edges of lower back bodies between dots. Stitch lower back bodies together J-L (through X and Y), leaving open between dots.

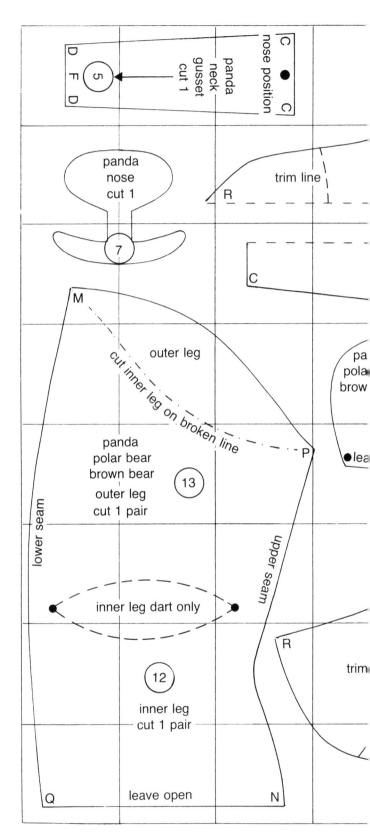

Pattern 1 for panda, polar bear, brown b

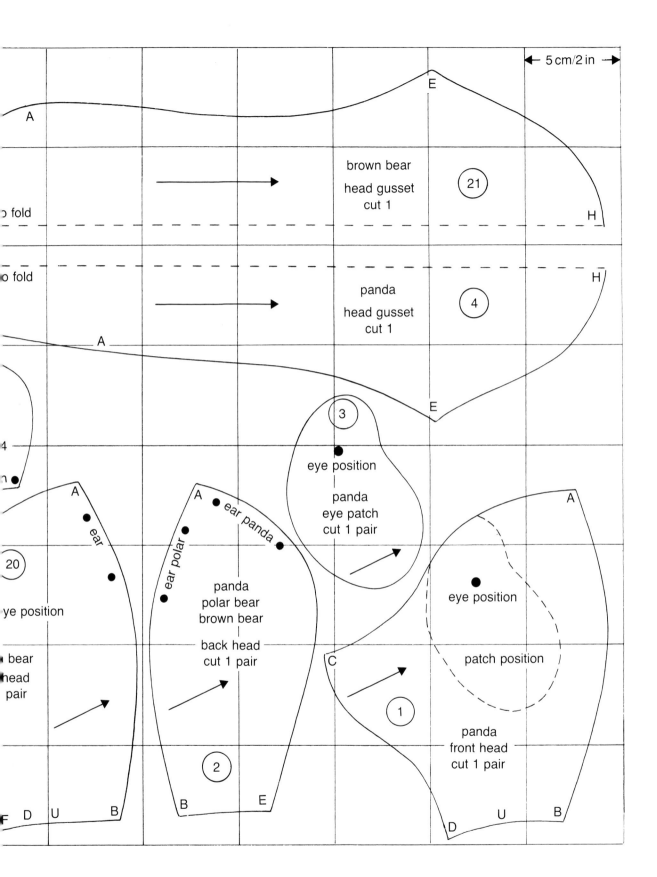

A

← 5 cm/2 in →

E

brown bear
head gusset
cut 1

(21)

H

o fold

o fold

H

panda
head gusset
cut 1

(4)

A

E

(3)

● eye position

panda
eye patch
cut 1 pair

4

● A

● ear

(20)

ye position

bear
head
pair

A ● ear panda ●

● ear polar ●

panda
polar bear
brown bear

back head
cut 1 pair

A

● eye position

patch position

C

(1)

panda
front head
cut 1 pair

(2)

B

B E

D U

F D U B

D U B

5. Stitch upper front body to lower front body K-G-K.
6. Stitch upper back body to lower back body K-J-K.
7. Stitch front body to back body round arms and side seams E-K-P. Stitch front to back body between legs M-L-M.
8. Stitch darts in inner legs. Stitch inner leg to outer leg M-Q and P-N. Repeat for the second leg.
9. Stitch feet into legs, matching N-Q.
10. With right sides facing and inner legs to the front, stitch legs into body, matching P and M.

Second step — the head and ears.

11. Stitch a front head to a back head A-B. Repeat with the other two pieces.
12. Stitch the neck gusset to the head gusset C-C.
13. Stitch the head gusset to the front and back heads D-C-A-E.
14. Slip stitch the edges of both eye patches to the wrong side and sew patches to head at the marked positions. Make a small hole through the fabrics at the eye positions, insert each eye and secure.
15. With right sides facing, fit and stitch the head into the neck, matching F-D-U-B-E at the front bodies and E-H at the back bodies. Turn the panda through to the right side.

16

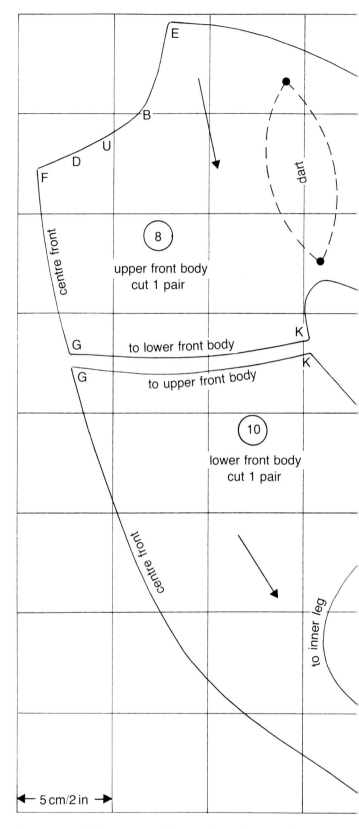

Pattern 2 for panda, polar bear, brown b

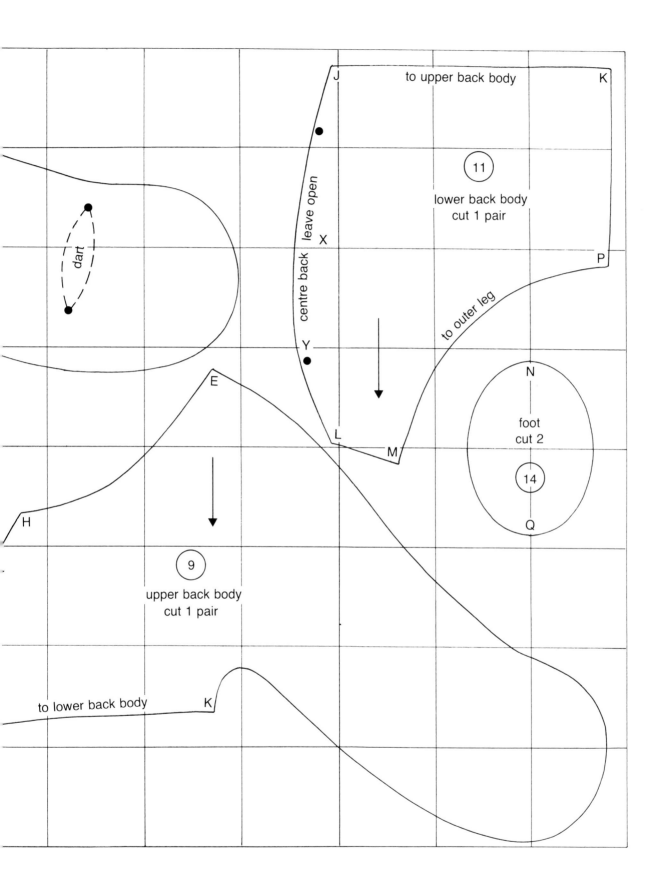

to upper back body

J

K

⑪

lower back body
cut 1 pair

dart

centre back   leave open

X

to outer leg

P

Y

N

foot
cut 2

E

L

M

⑭

Q

H

⑨

upper back body
cut 1 pair

to lower back body

K

16. Stitch darts in one pair (inner) ears. Stitch ears together in pairs, leaving the straight edge open. Turn to right side, fold in and slip stitch raw edges to inside.
17. Fill the panda, moulding the head to a good shape. Check that it will sit; add extra filling to the legs if necessary.
18. Turn in the edges of the gap and close using strong thread and ladder stitch.
19. Trim the fur pile round the nose. Sew the nose in position.
20. Sew the ears to the head.
21. To mould the face, use strong thread and a long needle to take stitches through the head from the inner corner of the eye to behind the ear.
22. Run a needle along seams to release any caught fur.

Brown bear

To make the brown bear, use the two patterns shown on pages 14–17. These should be drawn on to a 5 cms (2 ins) grid, to give a height of 46 cms (18 ins).

Materials

Medium pile dark brown fur fabric (pile to be stroked down towards the shorter length), 60 × 138 cms (23½ × 54¾ ins).
1 pair 21 mm brown safety eyes and washers.
1 30 mm black safety nose.
Pink yarn.
1 kg (2¼ lb) polyester filling.
Squared paper, 5 cms (2 ins).

Patterns

The following 11 pattern pieces are required, enlarged on to a 5 cms (2 ins) grid — back head No.2, ear No.6, upper front body No.8, upper back body No.9, lower front body No.10, lower back body No.11, inner leg No.12, outer leg No.13, foot No.14, front head No.20, head gusset No.21.

Cutting out

The seam allowance is 8 mm (⅓ in). Arrows indicate direction of pile.
Cut out the following pattern pieces:
From dark brown fur cut 1 pair front heads; 1 pair back heads; 1 head gusset; 4 ears; 1 pair upper front bodies; 1 pair upper back bodies; 1 pair lower front bodies; 1 pair lower back bodies; 1 pair inner legs; 1 pair outer legs; 2 feet.

To make

All seams are made with right sides facing.
First step — the body.
See panda instructions on page 14 and follow steps 1-10.
Second step — the head and ears.
11. Stitch a front head to a back head A-B. Repeat with the other two pieces.
12. Stitch the heads together R-F.
13. Stitch the head gusset to the heads R-A-E.
14. Trim fur pile to broken pattern line round mouth and nose. Make tiny holes in the fur fabric at the eye positions. Insert the eyes and secure with the washers. Make a small hole in the seam line at the nose dot, insert nose and secure. Embroider mouth.

To complete

To finish off the brown bear, see panda instructions on page 16 and follow steps 15-22.

Grizzly, or brown bears, are omniverous and they live chiefly in forests feeding on fruits and berries, fish, insects and small animals. Most bears like the taste of honey and when they can find it they will tear up a nest of wild bees with their large claws to reach the sweet-tasting honey inside! Although at one time they could be found in Europe, northern Asia and North America, today their numbers have dwindled and large populations can only be found in Canada, Alaska and the USSR.

Polar bear

To make the polar bear, use the three patterns shown on pages 14–17 and 22, 23. These should be drawn on to a 5 cms (2 ins) grid, to give a height of 46 cms (18 ins).

Materials

Medium pile white fur fabric (pile to be stroked down towards the shorter length), 60 × 137 cms (23½ × 54⅜ ins).
Black felt, 6 × 4 cms (2¼ × 1½ ins).
1 pair 21 mm blue safety eyes and washers.
Black yarn
1 kg (2¼ lb) polyester filling.
Handicraft glue.
Squared paper, 5 cms (2 ins).

Patterns

The following 14 pattern pieces are required, enlarged on to a 5 cms (2 ins) grid — back head No.2, ear No.6, upper front body No.8, upper back body No.9, lower front body No.10, lower back body No.11, inner leg No.12, outer leg No.13, foot No.14, front head No.15, neck gusset No.16, nose No.17, tail No. 18, head gusset No.19.

Cutting out

The seam allowance is 8 mm (⅓ in). Arrows indicate direction of pile.
Cut out the following pattern pieces:
From white fur fabric, cut 1 pair front heads; 1 pair back heads; 1 head gusset; 1 neck gusset; 4 ears; 1 pair upper front bodies; 1 pair upper back bodies; 1 pair lower front bodies; 1 pair lower back bodies; 1 pair inner legs; 1 pair outer legs; 2 feet; 1 pair tails.
Spread glue on to the back of the felt, allow to dry, then cut 1 nose.

To make

All seams are made with right sides facing.
First step — the body.
See panda instructions on page 14 and follow steps 1-10.

20

Second step — the head and ears.
11. Stitch darts in neck edges of front heads. Stitch front head to back head A-B. Repeat with other two pieces.
12. Stitch heads together S-T. Stitch head gusset to both head pieces S-A-E.
13. Stitch neck gusset to both front heads T-U.
14. Make a small hole through the fur fabric at the eye positions. Insert the eyes and secure with the washers.
15. With right sides facing, fit and stitch the head into the neck, matching F-D-U-B-E at the front bodies and E-H at the back bodies. Turn the polar bear through to the right side.
16. Stitch darts in one pair (inner) ears. Stitch ears together in pairs leaving the straight edges open. Turn to right side, fold in and slip stitch raw edges to inside.
17. Stitch the tails together, leaving open the straight edge X-Y. Turn tail to right side, fill lightly with stuffing and baste open edges together.
18. Turn in edges of the gap. Insert the tail between the open edges X-Y. With strong thread sew together the edges of the gap through the tail.
19. Trim fur pile round nose and mouth. Sew nose in position. Embroider mouth with yarn.
20. Fold ears along dart with inner ears facing. Sew ears to head.
21. To mould the face, use strong thread and a long needle to take stitches through the head from the inner corner of the eye to behind the ear.
22. Run a needle along seams to release any caught fur.

Polar bears live in the coastal regions of the cold, hostile Arctic and can travel great distances over the ice and snow hunting for food. They feed on seals, stranded whales, occasionally walruses, and they also eat birds, eggs and plant material when other food is unavailable. Their thick, white winter coats are water-repellent and serve as a protection against the cold as well as acting as an effective camouflage. No other land mammal lives so far north as the polar bear and many more people today are becoming interested in seeing this species preserved.

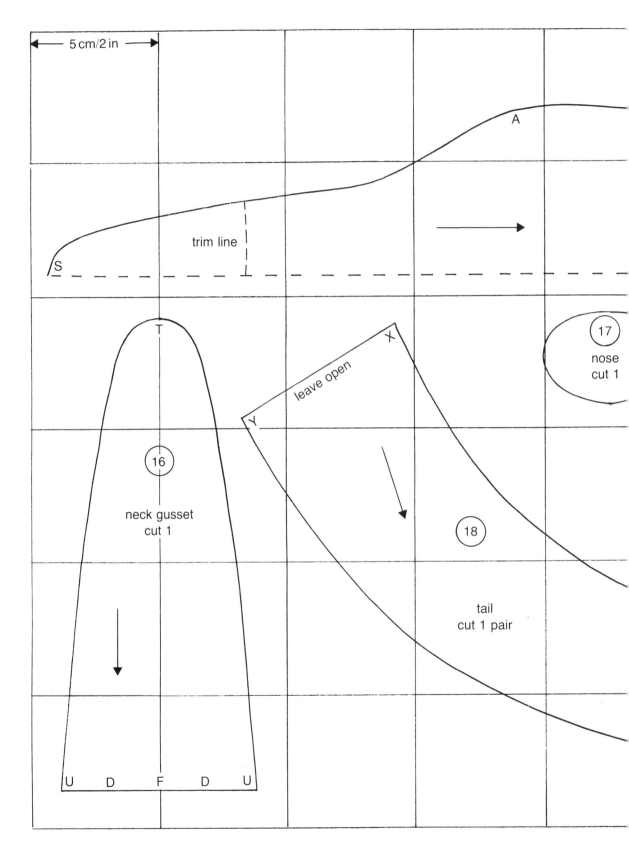

5 cm/2 in

A

trim line

S

T

17
nose
cut 1

leave open

X

Y

16

neck gusset
cut 1

18

tail
cut 1 pair

U   D   F   D   U

Pattern for polar bear

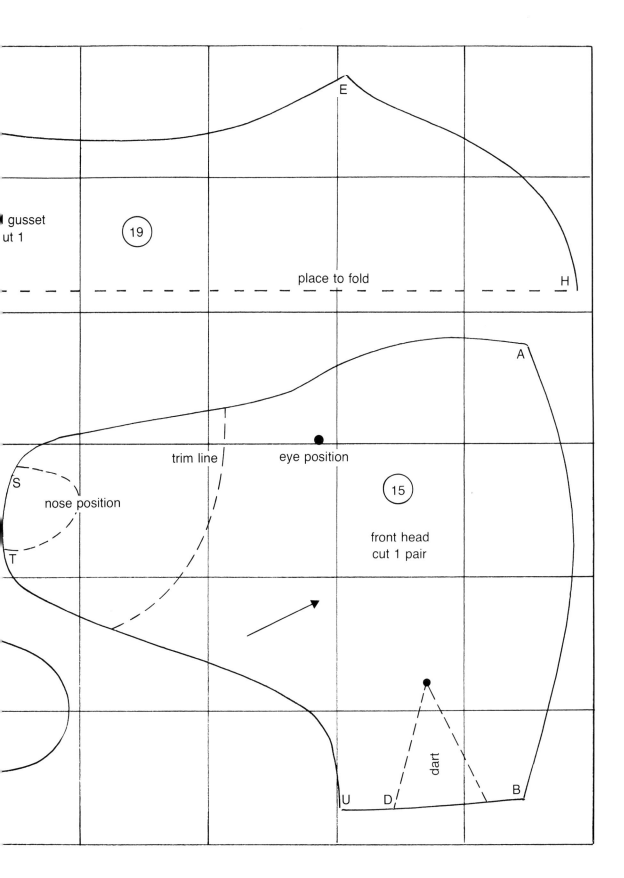

gusset
ut 1

(19)

place to fold

E

H

A

trim line

eye position

S

nose position

T

(15)

front head
cut 1 pair

dart

U   D

B

23

Lions, tigers & leopards

The lion, tiger and leopard are all adapted from the same basic body pattern, see pages 30–35, but different head patterns are used on each animal.

Lion

To make the lion, use the patterns shown on the above pages. These should be drawn on to a 5 cms (2 ins) grid, to give a length of 51 cms (20 ins) without the tail.

Materials

Honey short pile polished fur fabric, 60 × 137 cms (23½ × 54 ins).
Honey long pile fur fabric (the pile to be stroked down towards the shorter length of both furs), 30 × 60 cms (11¾ × 23½ ins).
1 pair 21 mm amber safety eyes.
Black double knitting yarn.
22 white plastic safety whiskers.
Black and white permanent waterproof marking pens.
700 gm (1½ lb) polyester filling.
Squared paper, 5 cms (2 ins).

Patterns

The following 14 pattern pieces are required, enlarged on to a 5 cms (2 ins) grid — front head No.1, front head gusset No.2, back head No.3, back head gusset No.4, neck gusset No. 5, inner ear No.6, outer ear No.7, body No. 8, underbody No.9, upper rear leg No.10, chest No.11, foot No.12, tail No.13, tail tuft No.14.

Cutting out

The seam allowance is 8 mm (⅓ in). Arrows indicate direction of pile.
Cut out the following pattern pieces:
From short pile fur cut 1 pair bodies; 1 pair underbodies; 1 pair upper rear legs; 4 feet; 1 tail; 1 pair front heads; 1 front head gusset; 1 neck gusset; 2 inner ears.

From long pile fur cut 1 chest; 1 tail tuft; 1 pair back heads; 1 back head gusset; 2 outer ears.

To make

All seams are made with right sides facing.
First step — the body.
1. Stitch bodies together D-E and F-Q, leaving open E-F for the tail.
2. Oversew straight edges of underbodies between dots to prevent stretching. Stitch darts in underbodies at legs.
3. Stitch underbodies together H-Q leaving open between dots.
4. Stitch chest to underbodies G-H-G.
5. Stitch underbodies to bodies at rear C-Q-C.
6. Stitch darts in upper rear legs.
7. Stitch upper rear legs to body matching A-B-C, and also to the underbody from C-N.
8. Continue to stitch the underbodies to the body from M (rear foot)-A-P-L (front foot) and from K-G-J (at the upper edge of the chest), leaving open the feet K-L and M-N.
9. Stitch the tail tuft to the tail, matching the dots. Fold the tail along the centre length

The lion's strength, predatory habits and regal appearance have earned it the name 'King of the Beasts' or 'Lord of the Jungle'. In fact, lions do not live in the jungle, they live in family groups, or prides, in the open grasslands of Africa and a small area of India. The prides hunt together and it is usually the lionesses who chase and kill the prey. Although the lion is now an endangered species, still hunters are drawn to Africa, eager for a trophy which proves their supremacy over this animal.

E-R. Stitch together F-R leaving open straight edges E-F. Turn tail through to the right side. Baste open edges together. With right sides facing, insert the tail into the body matching E and F. Baste and stitch bodies together (through all layers) from E-F.

10. Stitch the front feet into the legs K-L.
11. Stitch the rear feet into the legs M-N.

Second step — the head and ears.
12. Stitch darts in inner ears.
13. Stitch one inner ear to one outer ear leaving open straight edges. Turn ear to right side. Make second ear.
14. Bring the open edges of the back head S-T together, matching S-S. Stitch seam S-T. Taper the seam at T.
15. Stitch darts in back head neck edges.
16. Stitch darts in front heads. Match W-W at each mouth. Stitch seams W-X, tapering the seams at X.
17. Stitch front heads to back heads Z-Y.
18. Stitch front head gusset to neck gusset I-I.
19. Stitch front head gusset to back head gusset Z-Z.
20. Stitch front and neck gussets to front and back heads V-Y-O-W-I-Z-U. Turn head through to right side.
21. Make a slit hole in the fur at the eye positions. Push the safety eyes through the fur from the right side and fix with the washers.
22. With black yarn and straight stitches embroider the nose and mouth.
23. Push individual whiskers through the fur from the wrong side. Add a little filling to the nose to keep the whiskers in place.
24. With right sides facing, insert the head into the body through the neck. With raw edges even, match the neck V-J-U-D on both sides of the neck edge. Baste and stitch the head to the body. Turn body through to right side.
25. Fill the head, neck and limbs with stuffing, then add filling to the body. It should remain floppy and cuddly.
26. Turn in the raw edges of the gap and sew together to enclose filling.

26

27. Turn in raw edges of ears and stitch to head on seams S-T between dots, with the inner ear to the front.
28. With strong thread and a long needle take stitches through the front head gusset, on the dots, to model the nose.
29. Mark the inner and outer corners of the fur round the eyes with the black pen. Try the pen on scrap fur before marking toy. With the white pen mark the side edges of the fur round the eyes and the chin.
30. Brush fur well and run a needle along the seams to release any caught fur.

Tiger

To make the tiger, use the patterns shown on pages 30–35. These should be drawn on to a 5 cms (2 ins) grid, to give a length of 51 cms (20 ins) without the tail.

Materials

Tiger fur fabric (extra fabric required for matching stripes), 70 × 137 cms (27½ × 54 ins).
Soft white fur (pile to be stroked down towards the shorter length of both fabrics), 30 × 40 cms (11¾ × 15¾ ins).
Flesh pink felt, 5 × 5 cms (2 × 2 ins).
1 pair 21 mm amber safety eyes.

Few animals evoke such fear and admiration as the tiger. They are the largest of the feline species and include the Siberian tiger, the Caspian tiger and the Bengal tiger. They are found only in Asia, from India to China and Indonesia and all members of this family are now endangered. Their habitat includes tropical and snow-covered forests, mangrove swamps and drier forest areas.
They are carnivores and employ various methods of maintaining rights to their territory. A killing bite is delivered by long, flattened canines and they can easily carry large prey in their massive jaws.

22 white safety whiskers.
Black double knitting yarn.
700 gm (1½ lb) polyester filling.
Black permanent marking pen.
Squared paper, 5 cms (2 ins).

Patterns

The following 15 pattern pieces are required, enlarged on to a 5 cms (2 ins) grid — front head No.1, front head gusset No.2, back head No.3, back head gusset No.4, neck gusset No.5, body No.8, underbody No.9, upper rear leg No.10, chest No.11, foot No.12, eye patch No.15, inner ear No.16, outer ear No.17, nose No.18, tail No.19.

Cutting out

The seam allowance is 8 mm (⅓ in). Arrows indicate direction of pile.
From tiger fur cut 1 front head gusset; 1 pair back heads; 1 back head gusset; 1 pair eye patches; 2 outer ears; 1 pair bodies; 1 pair underbodies; 4 feet; 1 pair upper rear legs; 1 pair tails.
From white fur cut 1 pair front heads; 1 neck gusset; 1 chest; 2 inner ears.
From pink felt cut 1 nose.

To make

All seams are made right sides facing.
First step — the body.
See lion instructions on page 24 and follow steps 1-8.

9. Stitch tail pieces together leaving open straight edges E-F. Turn tail through to right side; add a little filling to the tail. Baste open edges together. With right sides facing insert tail into the body, matching E and F. Baste and stitch bodies together through all layers from E-F.
10-11. See lion pattern.
Second step — the head and ears.
12-15. See lion pattern.
16. Stitch darts in front heads, trim fur pile to dotted line. Match W-W at each mouth. Stitch seams W-X, tapering the seams at X.
17-20. See lion pattern.

28

21. Place the eye patches on to the head. Turn under the raw edges and slip stitch the patches to the fur.
22. Make a tiny hole in the fur at the eye positions. Push the safety eyes through the fur from the right side and fix with the washers.
23-27. See lion pattern.
28. Mark a black dot at the base of each whisker with the pen, and mark the nostrils on to the felt nose. Try the pen on scrap fur before marking the toy.
29. Sew the nose in position. Embroider the mouth with yarn.
30. Brush the fur well and run a needle along the seams to release any caught fur.

Leopard

To make the leopard, use the patterns shown on pages 30 – 35. These should be drawn on to a 5 cms (2 ins) grid, to give a length of 51 cms (20 ins) without the tail.

Materials

Leopard fur fabric, 80 × 137 cms (31½ × 54 ins).
Tan felt, 5 × 6 cms (2 × 2¼ ins)
Cream felt, 5 × 5 cms (2 × 2 ins)
1 pair 18 mm yellow cats' safety eyes.
30 mm black plastic safety nose.
22 black plastic safety whiskers.
700 gm (1½ lb) polyester filling
Squared paper, 5 cms (2 ins)

Patterns

The following 15 pattern pieces are required, enlarged on to a 5 cms (2 ins) grid — front head gusset No.2, back head No.3, back head gusset No.4, inner ear No.6, outer ear No.7, body No.8, underbody No.9, upper rear leg No.10, chest No.11, foot No.12, tail No.19, front head No.20, neck gusset No.21, outer eye patch No.22, inner eye patch No.23.

The leopard is one of the five species of the genus Panthera and is now threatened with extinction. Its spotted coat, with distinctive black spots on a fawn to pale brown background, has played a large part in its decline, as it is highly prized by furriers. It is found in Africa, south of the Sahara and in South Asia, with scattered populations in North Africa, Arabia and the Far East, and its habitat ranges from tropical rain forests to arid savanna.

It is a carnivore, preferring to lie in wait in a tree, or amongst suitable cover, as the spots on its coat provide excellent camouflage. The prominent sensitive whiskers are those of an animal that hunts at night.

Cutting out

The seam allowance is 8 mm (⅓ in).
Arrows indicate direction of pile.
From leopard fur cut 1 pair front heads; 1 pair back heads; 1 front head gusset; 1 back head gusset; 1 neck gusset; 1 pair inner ears; 1 pair outer ears; 1 pair bodies; 1 pair underbodies; 1 pair upper back legs; 1 chest; 4 feet; 1 pair tails.
From tan felt cut 2 outer eye patches.
From cream felt cut 2 inner eye patches.

To make

All seams are made with right sides facing.

First step — the body
See lion instructions on page 24 and follow steps 1-8.

9. Stitch tail pieces together, leaving open straight edges E-F. Turn tail through to right side. Add a little filling and baste open edges together. With right sides facing insert the tail into the body matching E and F. Baste and stitch bodies together through all layers E-F.

10-11. See lion pattern.

Second step — the head and ears

12-15. See lion pattern.

16. Omit

17-20. See lion pattern.

21. Make a tiny slit in the centre of each eye patch and the fur fabric at the eye positions. Place the tan eye patch, with the cream patch on top, on to the fur fabric. Insert the eye stalks through the three layers and secure with the washers.

22. Make a slit in the fabric for the nose. Insert and secure the nose. Embroider the mouth.

23-27. See lion pattern.

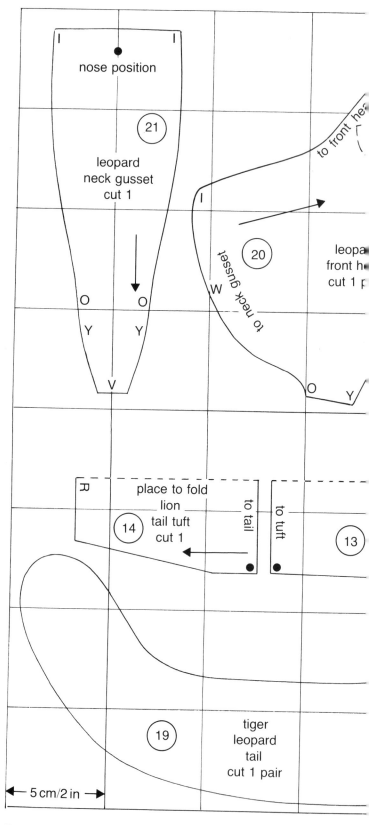

Pattern 1 for lion, tiger and leopard

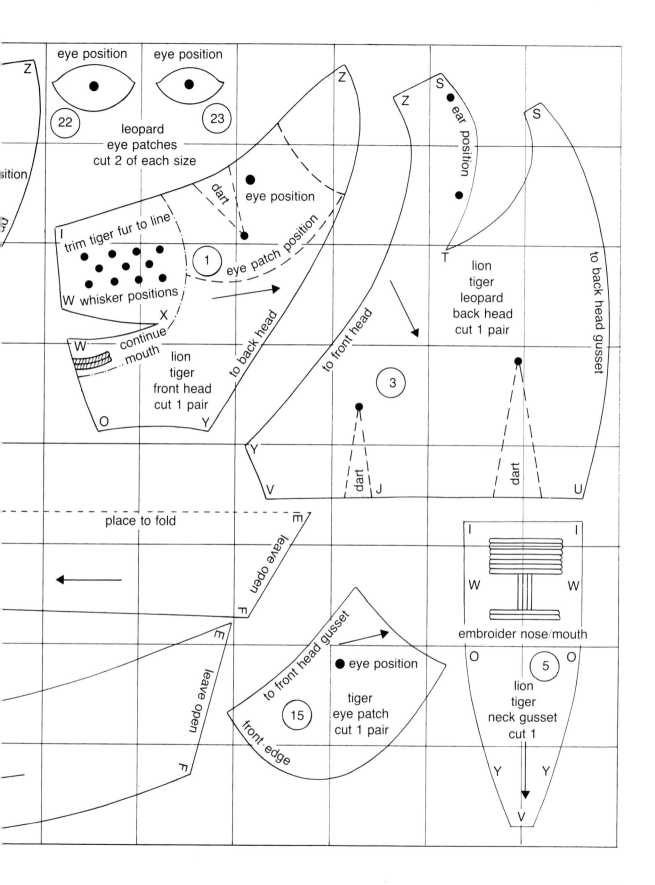

eye position

eye position

22

23

leopard
eye patches
cut 2 of each size

eye position

dart

trim tiger fur to line

eye patch position

1

W whisker positions

to back head

continue
mouth

lion
tiger
front head
cut 1 pair

O

Y

Z

Z

S

ear position

S

T

lion
tiger
leopard
back head
cut 1 pair

to back head gusset

to front head

3

dart

J

dart

U

V

Y

place to fold

leave open

m

F

E

leave open

F

to front head gusset

eye position

tiger
eye patch
cut 1 pair

15

front edge

embroider nose/mouth

I

I

W

W

O

O

5

lion
tiger
neck gusset
cut 1

Y

Y

V

31

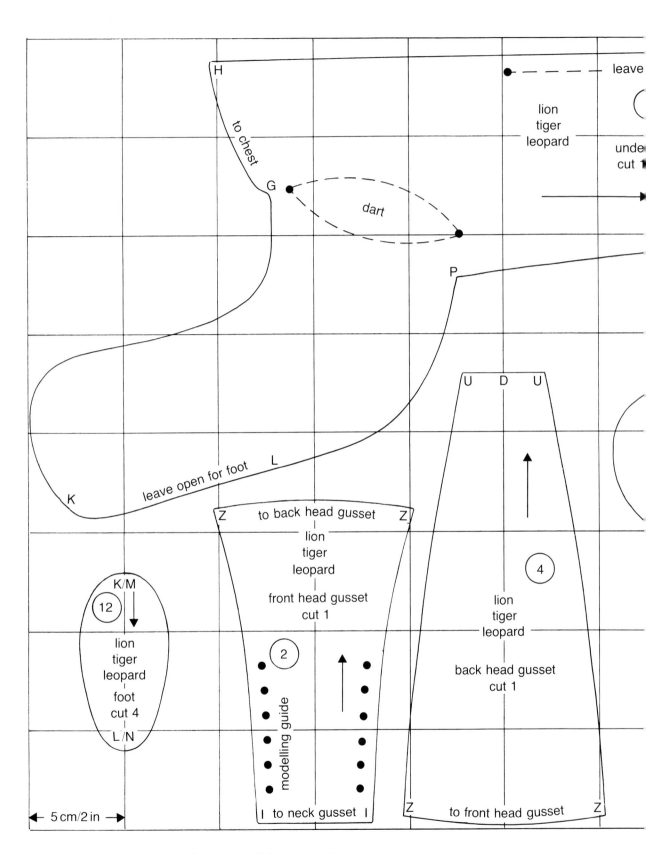

H

to chest

G

dart

P

leave

lion
tiger
leopard

unde
cut 1

U D U

leave open for foot

L

K

Z to back head gusset Z

lion
tiger
leopard

front head gusset
cut 1

4

lion
tiger
leopard

back head gusset
cut 1

K/M

12

lion
tiger
leopard

foot
cut 4

L/N

2

modelling guide

Z to front head gusset Z

I to neck gusset I

← 5 cm/2 in →

Pattern 2 for lion, tiger and leopard

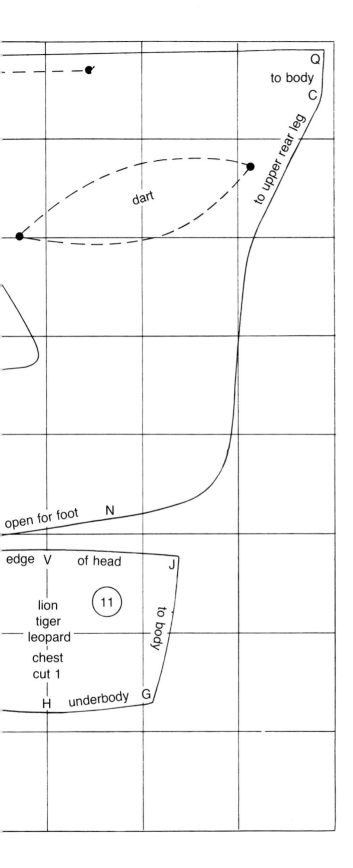

Q
to body
C
to upper rear leg

dart

open for foot N

edge V of head J

lion
tiger
leopard
chest
cut 1

(11)

to body

H underbody G

28. With strong thread and a long needle take stitches from the inner corner of the eye to behind the opposite ear on each side. Take several stitches across the front head gusset to model the nose.

29. Brush fur well and run a needle along the seams to release any caught fur.

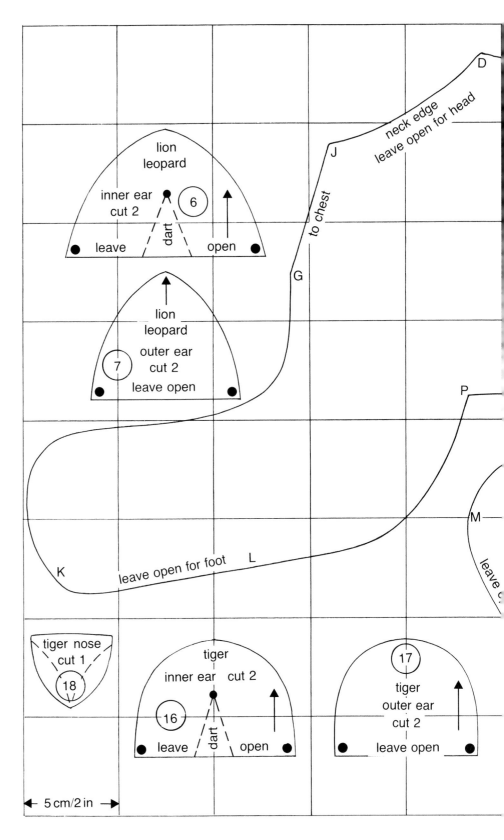

Pattern 3 for lion, tiger and leopard

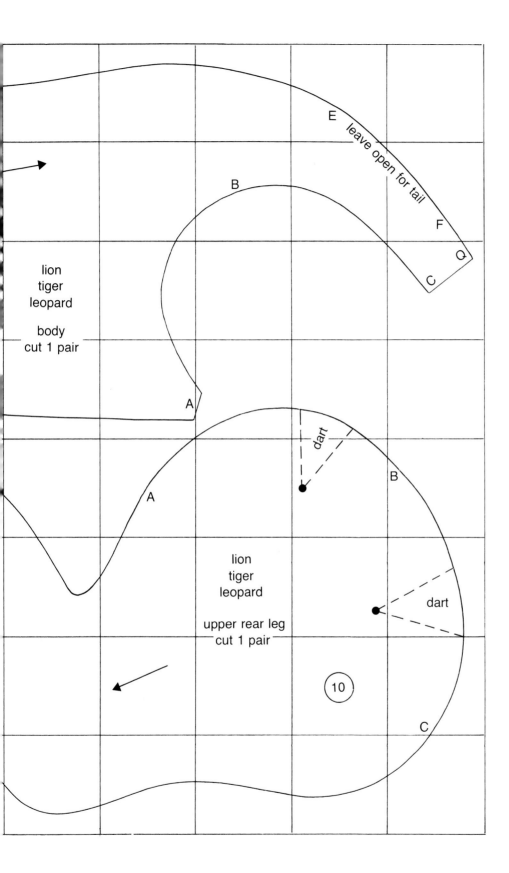

E leave open for tail

F

Q

C

B

A

lion
tiger
leopard

body
cut 1 pair

A

dart

B

dart

lion
tiger
leopard

upper rear leg
cut 1 pair

10

C

35

Elephants

To make the large and small elephants, use the pattern shown on page 39. The pattern for the large elephant should be drawn on to a 5 cms (2 ins) grid to give a height of 33 cms (13 ins); the pattern for the small elephant should be drawn on to a 2.5 cms (1 in) grid to give a height of 17 cms (6¾ ins).

Materials

For one large and one small elephant:
Dark grey short pile polished fur fabric, 60 × 138 cms (23½ × 54¾ ins).
Light grey short pile polished fur fabric (the pile to be stroked down towards the shorter length of both furs), 30 × 40 cms (11¾ × 15¾ ins).
Light grey felt, 6 × 8 cms (2¼ × 3¼ ins).
1 pair of 21 mm brown and 1 pair of 16 mm safety eyes and washers.
1 kg (2¼ lb) polyester filling.
Black double knitting yarn.
Squared paper, 5 cms (2 ins) and 2.5 cms (1 in).

Patterns

The following 10 pattern pieces are required, enlarged on to a 5 cms (2 ins) grid for the large elephant and on to a 2.5 cms (1 in) grid for the small elephant — body, underbody, head gusset, neck gusset, nose, eye patch, mouth, ear, tail, foot.

Cutting out

The seam allowance is 8 mm (⅓ in) for the large elephant and 5 mm (⅕ in) for the small elephant. Arrows indicate direction of pile.
For each elephant cut out the following pattern pieces:
From dark grey fur cut 1 pair bodies; 1 pair underbodies; 1 head gusset; 1 neck gusset; 1 tail; 1 mouth; 1 pair ears; 4 feet.
From light grey fur cut 1 pair ears; 1 mouth; 1 nose.
From light grey felt cut 2 eye patches.
Trim the fur pile of the feet and nose.

36

Elephants are herbivores and are the largest known l animals. They are found in two regions; the biggest i African elephant found south of the Sahara and can recognized by its huge, flattened ears. The smaller Ind or Asiatic species, found in India, Indochina , Malaysi southern China, has small ears which fold over at the The Indian elephant is already an endangered species the African is now also very vulnerable.

To make

All seams are made with right sides facing.
First step — the body.
1. Stitch body darts at the trunk and rump.
2. Stitch the head gusset to both sides of the body A-B-C.

3. Stitch the trunks together A-D. Stitch the centre back seam of body C through T to E.

4. Oversew each underbody centre seam edge between dots to prevent stretching. Stitch darts above legs.

5. Stitch underbodies together F-E, leaving open between dots.

6. Stitch neck gusset to underbody G-F-G.

7. Stitch neck gusset and underbody to the body D-H-G-J. Stitch the underbody to the

body K-L and M-E, leaving open for the feet J-K and L-M.

8. Stitch feet into legs J-K and L-M (for the small elephant this seam is easier to sew by hand using back stitch and double sewing thread).
9. Turn the body through to the right side.
10. Stitch one light (inner) ear to one dark ear leaving open edges N-P-N-Q. Repeat. Turn ears to right side; fold in seam allowance on raw edges to inside and slip stitch open edges together.
11. Stitch darts in tail. For the large elephant — with right sides facing fold tail along centre length and stitch edges and narrow end together, leaving open at T. Turn tail to right side. For the small elephant — with wrong sides facing fold the tail along centre of length, fold seam allowance to wrong side except at edge T. By hand sew the two folded edges together leaving open raw edges at T.

Second step — the head.

12. Stitch light (upper) mouth to dark mouth leaving open straight edges H-H. Turn to right side, fold in raw edges and baste together.
13. Cut a tiny slit in the centre of each eye patch, place each in position. Make another slit in the fur to match. Push safety eyes through the slits; secure with washers.
14. Lightly fill the trunk, then fill the legs, head and body firmly. Turn in the raw edges of the opening and slip stitch together to enclose the filling.
15. Add a little filling to the tail. Turn in raw edges and stitch tail firmly to the rump at T, with the seam towards the underbody.
16. Fold the ears at P, (inner ears facing), matching N-N. Sew ears to body P-Q.
17. Sew the mouth to the elephant H-H, with the light fur facing the chin gusset.
18. Fold 3 mm (⅛ in) of nose edge to the wrong side and sew it to end of trunk.
19. With yarn and straight stitches embroider the smiling mouth and nostrils.
20. Brush fur well and run a needle along seams to release any caught fur.

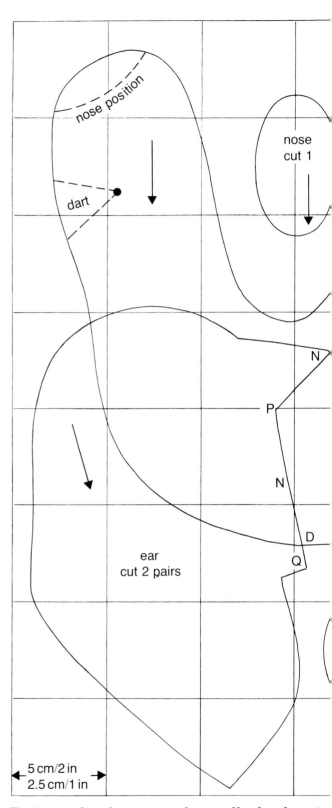

Pattern for large and small elephant

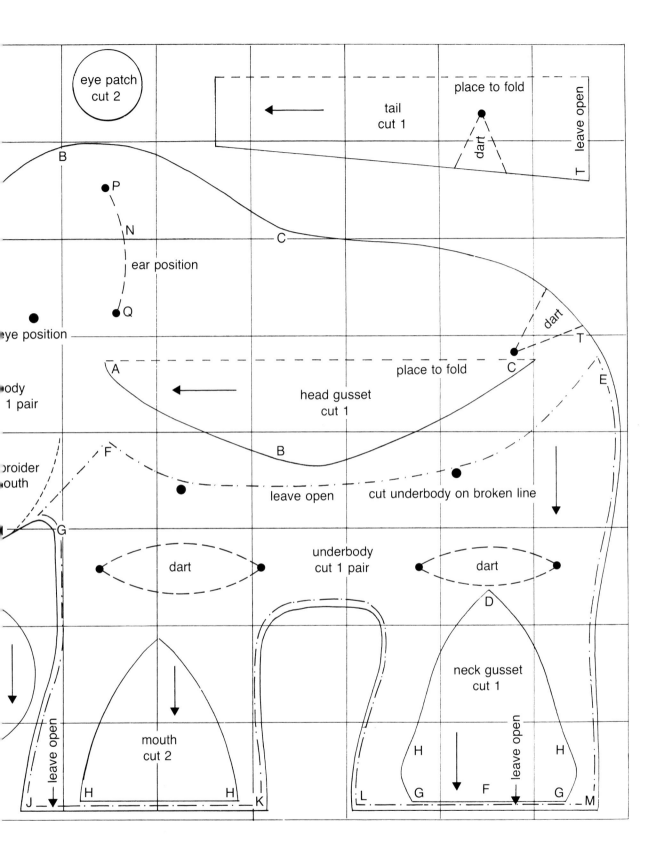

eye patch
cut 2

tail
cut 1

place to fold

leave open

dart

T

B

P

N

ear position

Q

eye position

A

body
1 pair

place to fold

head gusset
cut 1

C

T

C

E

embroider
mouth

F

B

leave open

cut underbody on broken line

G

dart

underbody
cut 1 pair

dart

D

neck gusset
cut 1

leave open

leave open

H

H

mouth
cut 2

H

H

I

J

K

L

G

F

G

M

Monkeys

The same pattern pieces are used for the large and small monkeys. The orang-outang is also made out of the same pattern pieces, but long pile chestnut fabric fur is used in place of brown fur fabric.

Large monkey

To make the large monkey, use the patterns shown on pages 43 and 45. These are drawn on to a 5 cms (2 ins) grid to give a height of 55 cms (21¾ ins).

Materials

Short pile polished dark brown fur fabric, 50 × 150 cms (19¾ × 60 ins).
Velvet pile mink fur fabric (the pile to be stroked down towards the shorter length of both fabrics), 30 × 77 cms (11¾ × 30¼ ins).
1 pair 16 mm black safety eyes.
Black double knitting yarn.
450 gm (1 lb) polyester filling.
Squared paper, 5 cms (2 ins).

Patterns

The following 15 pattern pieces are required, enlarged on to a 5 cms (2 ins) grid — head, head gusset, face, mouth, ear, body, front body, base, tail, inner arm, outer arm, hand, inner leg, outer leg, foot.

Cutting out

The seam allowance is 8 mm (⅓ in). Arrows indicate direction of pile.
From dark brown fur cut 1 pair heads; 1 head gusset; 1 pair bodies; 1 front body; 1 pair inner legs; 1 pair outer legs; 1 pair inner arms; 1 pair outer arms; 1 base; 1 pair tails.
From mink fur cut 1 pair faces; 1 mouth; 2 pairs ears; 2 pairs hands; 2 pairs feet.

To make

All seams are made with right sides facing.
1. Stitch face pieces together A-B. Stitch mouth to faces C-B-C
2. Stitch neck dart in heads. Stitch head gusset to heads D-E. Stitch face to head matching A-D-F-C-K on both sides. Turn head through to right side.
3. With matching sewing thread machine stitch round broken line on one pair of ears to make the inner ears. Stitch one inner ear to one outer ear leaving straight edges open. Turn ears through to right side, turn in raw edges and baste.
4. Stitch centre back seam of bodies H-J through S and N, leaving open between dots.
5. Stitch dart in front body. Stitch front body to both side edges of body K-L. With right sides facing, insert, baste and stitch the head on to the neck opening, matching K-M-K on the front body and K-E-H-K on the bodies.

The term 'monkey' covers a whole species of animals known as primates, who are similar in appearance and in their lifestyle. Old World primates come from Asia and Africa and New World monkeys live in the tropical rain forests of America. This group varies in size from the gorilla to the marmoset, both of which are now endangered species. It also includes man's nearest cousin, the chimpanzee.

Monkeys eat small insects and fruits and it is possible for several different species to co-exist, as they feed off different layers of the tree canopies.

6. Stitch the base to the lower edges of the bodies Q-J-Q and to front body P-P.

7. Stitch inner legs to outer legs W-R and L-T, leaving open short edges at both ends of legs W-L and R-T. Turn legs to right side. Insert, baste and stitch legs into the body and base matching L (front seams)-Q-W (rear seams)-P. Turn body through to right side.

8. Machine stitch along broken lines on upper feet. Cut slit in upper feet. Stitch upper foot to lower foot, turn to right side through slit, fill lightly with stuffing and oversew open edges of slit to enclose stuffing. With matching sewing thread stitch through all layers, on broken lines, to mark toes and base of thumb.

9. Stitch darts in upper edges of outer arms. Stitch outer arm to inner arm leaving open straight wrist edge X-Y. Turn arms through to right side.

10. Stitch darts in one pair (inner) hands. Stitch inner to outer hand leaving open straight edge X-Y. Turn hand through to right side; fill lightly with stuffing and baste open edges together. Stitch fingers and base of thumb as for feet. Repeat.

11. Stitch tail pieces together, leaving open straight edges S-N. Turn tail to right side.

12. Make a small hole in the face fabric at the eye positions. Insert the safety eyes and secure with washers.

13. Embroider nose with small straight stitches.

14. Fill the head with stuffing, moulding it to a good shape. Lightly fill the legs leaving a gap in the stuffing where the legs meet the body. Fill the body and oversew the open edges to enclose the stuffing.

15. Turn in the raw edges of the legs and sew a foot to each leg with the toes facing inwards.

16, Fill upper arms firmly and lower arms slightly. Insert and sew hands into arms matching X and Y.

17. Sew upper arms to body.

18. Sew ears to head with inner ear to the front.

19. Turn in raw edges of tail and sew to body matching S and N.

20. Brush fur well and run a needle along seams to release any caught fur.

Small monkey

To make the small monkey, use the patterns shown on pages 43 and 45. These are drawn on to a 2.5 cms (1 in) grid to give a height of 28 cms (11 ins).

Materials

Short pile polished dark brown fur fabric (the pile to be stroked down towards the shorter length), 30 × 80 cms (11¾ × 31½ ins).
Mink felt, 2 squares of 23 × 23 cms (9 × 9 ins).
1 pair 9 mm black safety eyes and washers.
Black embroidery thread.
100 gm (4 oz) polyester filling.
Squared paper, 2.5 cms (1 in).

Patterns

The pattern pieces are the same as those required for the large monkey (see page 40), enlarged on to a 2.5 cms (1 in) grid.

Cutting out

The seam allowance is 5 mm (⅕ in). Arrows indicate direction of pile.
Cut out all brown fur fabric pieces, following the instructions on page 40 for the large monkey. Cut out all mink pieces as for the large monkey using felt in place of mink fur fabric.

To make

All seams are made with right sides facing.
First step — the body.
See instructions for the large monkey on page 40 and follow steps 1-7.

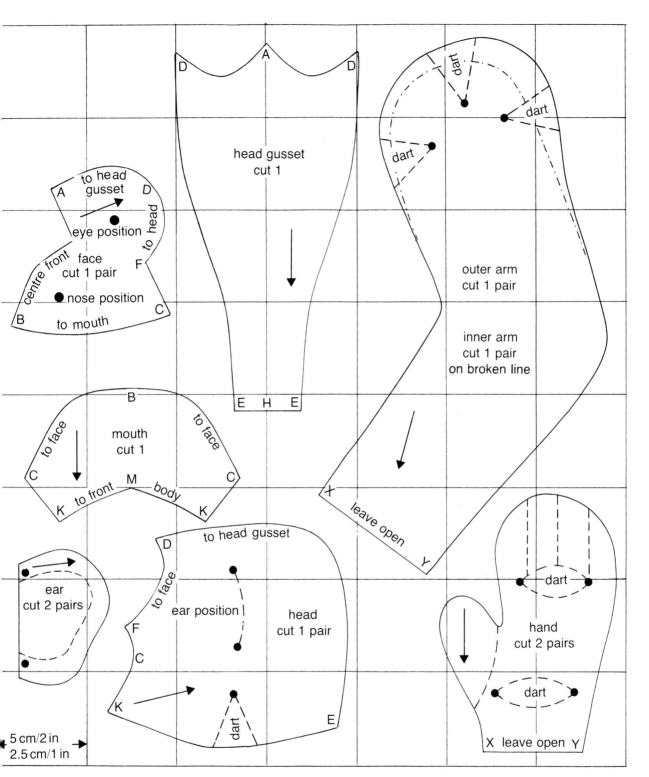

attern 1 for large and small monkey

8. Machine stitch round broken lines on upper feet. Cut slit in upper feet. With wrong sides facing, stitch inner to outer foot with 3 mm (⅛ in) top stitched seams. Add a scrap of filling, oversew edges of slit. Continue as for large monkey.

9. Stitch darts in inner hands. With wrong sides facing, stitch inner to outer hand as for foot, leaving open straight edges X-Y. Add a little filling and oversew open edges to enclose stuffing. Stitch fingers and thumb.

10. Complete the small monkey as for the large monkey.

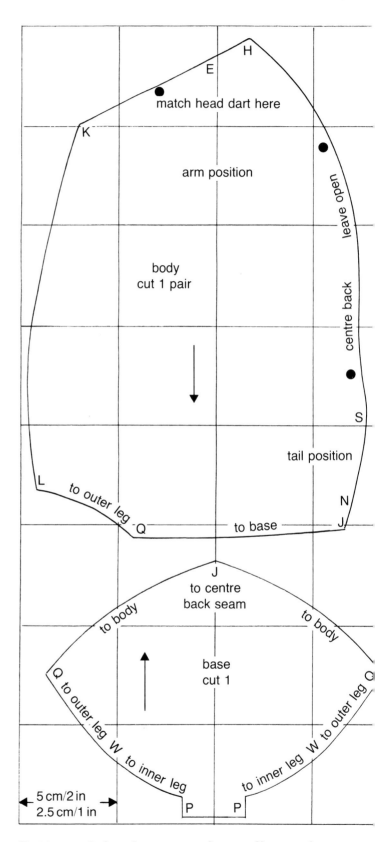

Pattern 2 for large and small monkey

44

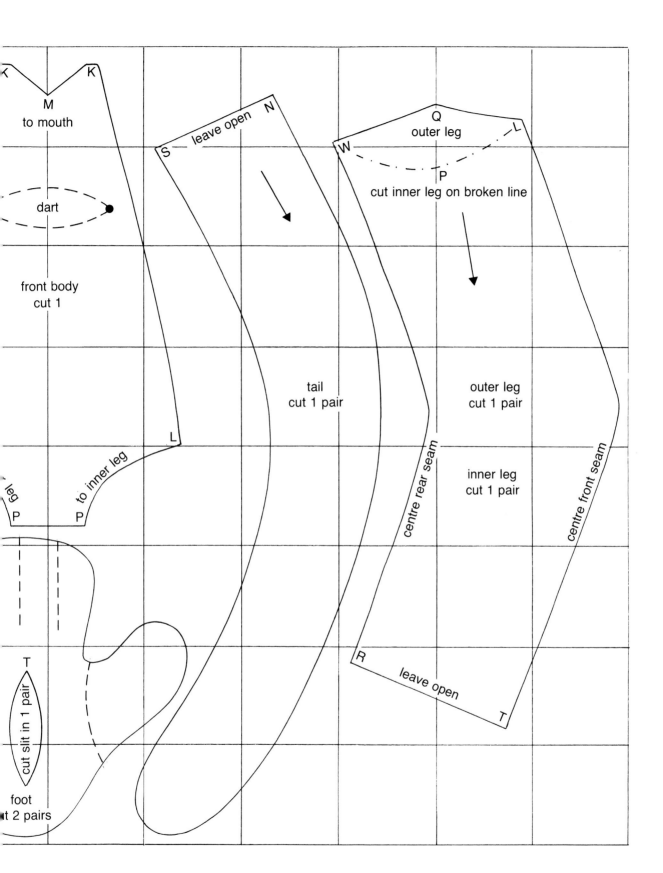

K

K

M
to mouth

dart

front body
cut 1

leave open   N

S

tail
cut 1 pair

L

to inner leg

leg

P   P

T

cut slit in 1 pair

foot
cut 2 pairs

Q   outer leg
W   L

P
cut inner leg on broken line

outer leg
cut 1 pair

centre rear seam

inner leg
cut 1 pair

centre front seam

R
leave open
T

45

Orang-Outang

To make the Orang-Outang, use the patterns for the large monkey shown on pages 43 and 45. These are drawn on to a 5 cms (2 ins) grid to give a height of 55 cms (21¾ ins).

Materials

All materials are as for the large monkey, (see page 40), using long pile chestnut fur fabric in place of brown fur fabric. *Long pile fur fabric should not be used to make a toy for a young child, who may suck and swallow the hair.*
You will also require a strong cream thread and a brown waterproof marker pen.

Patterns and cutting out

As for the large monkey, omitting the tail.

To make

To make up follow the instructions for the large monkey.
After the toy is completed, mould the face. Use strong thread and a long needle and take two stitches through the face at C. Pull the thread slightly to mould the mouth and fasten thread. To accentuate the eyes, mark the fur fabric round each corner and the outer edge with the pen; also mark the mouth and toe nails.
Try the pen on scrap fabric before using on the toy.

The shy orang-outang, or 'Man of the Woods' is found only in the rain forests of Sumatra and Borneo. It was once widespread throughout South East Asia but is now in danger of extinction because of the indiscriminate clearance of the forests.
The male grows to a body length of about 97 cm/38 in and has exceptionally long arms and hook-shaped hands and feet. They spend most of their time in the trees and are able to reach across quite large gaps from one tree to the next. Their teeth and jaws are relatively large for tearing open and grinding coarse vegetation, hard nuts and tree bark.

First published in Great Britain 1989
Search Press Ltd.
Wellwood, North Farm Road,
Tunbridge Wells, Kent TN2 3DR

Copyright © Search Press Limited 1989

Photographs by Search Press Studios

No part of this book, text or illustration, may be
reproduced or transmitted in any form or by any means
by print, photoprint, microfilm, photocopier, or in any
way, known or as yet unknown, or stored in a retrieval
system, without written permission obtained beforehand
from Search Press.

The author and publishers would like to thank Notcutts
Garden Centre, Tonbridge Road, Pembury, for providing
some of the plants used in photography.

ISBN 0 85532 629 8

Typeset by Scribe Design, Gillingham, Kent
Made and printed in Spain by A.G. Elkar S. Coop, Bilbao-12